My Animal Friends

Copyright c 2021 by J. Terry Johnson. All rights reserved.

No part of this publication may be reproduced, stored in a retrieval system, or transmitted in any way by any means, electronic, mechanical, photocopy, recording or otherwise without the prior permission of the author except as provided by USA copyright law.

Published in the United States of America.

ISBN: 978-0-9884051-5-8

MY ANIMAL FRIENDS

IN THE TEXAS HILL COUNTRY

by

J. Terry Johnson

Illustrated by Alexandra Steward

Introduction

Listen to the stories of my animal friends that live and play in the Texas Hill Country. God has given them many gifts that make them special.

What gifts has God given you?

* * * * *

This book is dedicated to my seven grandchildren and now a whole new generation of great-grandchildren

Meet Arnie Armadillo. His skin is so thick, he looks like an army tank. Arnie's eyes are not strong, but his nose works well. He can smell food before he can see it.

Can you smell cookies baking in the oven?

Arnie's father can dig deep holes. He taught Arnie how to dig holes too. Arnie digs for food. He digs holes to sleep in and hides there when he is frightened.

God has given Arnie sharp claws to dig.

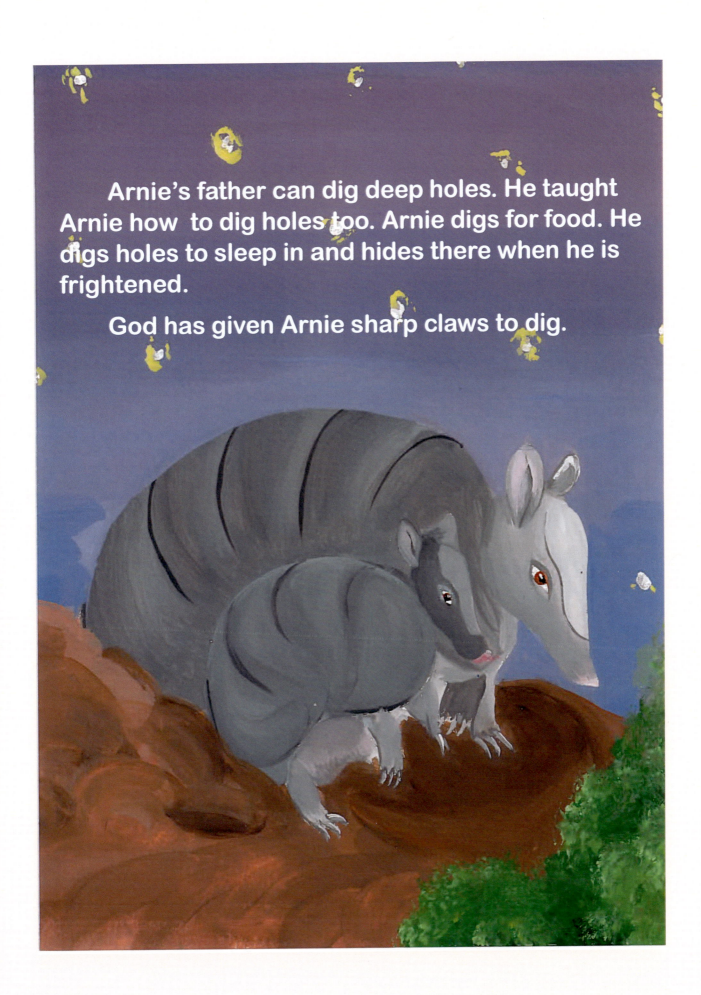

Debbie Deer is beautiful. She has big brown eyes and a brown fur coat. When she runs, her white tail sticks up in the air. Debbie Deer does not have antlers like her cousin Danny Deer.

Did God give you antlers?

Danny Deer likes to play with Debbie. They hunt for acorns and drink water from Pecan Creek. In the afternoon, they run and jump high over a fence.

Deer are good jumpers. God made them that way.

Henry Heron has long legs and a long neck. He has large wings and lots of feathers. When Henry walks, he slowly puts one foot in front of the other.

Can you walk like Henry?

Henry Heron loves the water. His grandfather taught Henry how to fish. He and his grandfather wade in the water and catch fish in their long beaks.

God gave Henry the patience to be a good fisherman.

Finis Fox looks like a red dog. He has four legs and a long, bushy tail. Finis is shy. He stays home in his den during the day and searches for his breakfast at night.

Do you like to play in the daytime or at night?

Finis and his sister Francine live in a hole dug beneath an old oak tree. When the moon is shining at night, they come out to play. They are sneaky and quiet to stay away from anyone who might hurt them.

God gives gifts to protect us from harm.

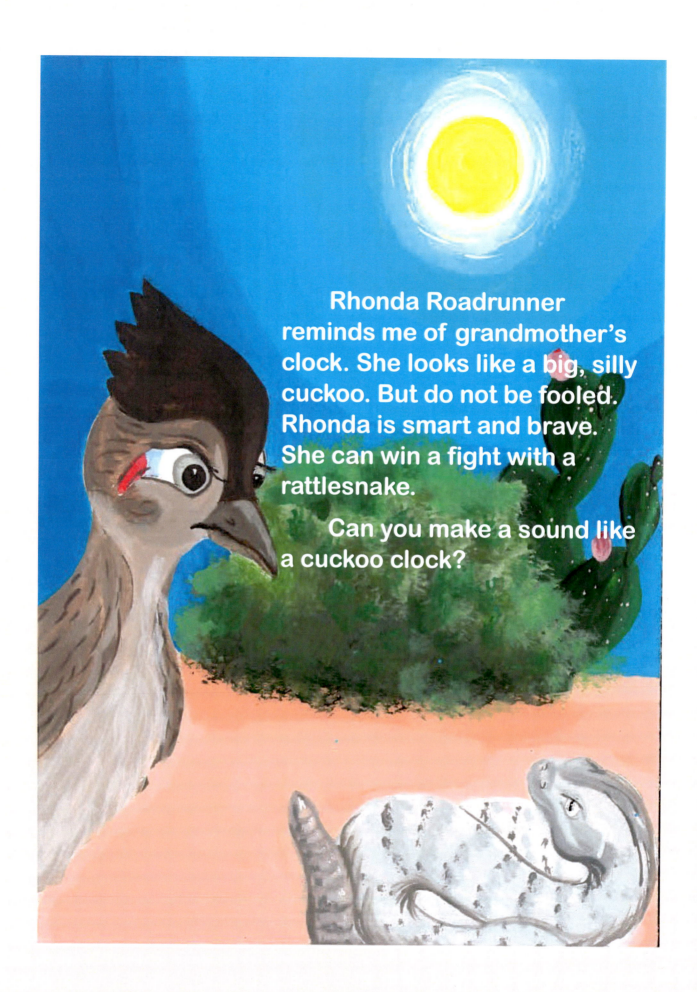

Rhonda Roadrunner reminds me of grandmother's clock. She looks like a big, silly cuckoo. But do not be fooled. Rhonda is smart and brave. She can win a fight with a rattlesnake.

Can you make a sound like a cuckoo clock?

When Rhonda Roadrunner's cousin Rachel comes for a visit, they explore the trails in the woods. Both are fast runners. They would rather run than fly like other birds do.

Being able to run fast is one of God's best gifts.

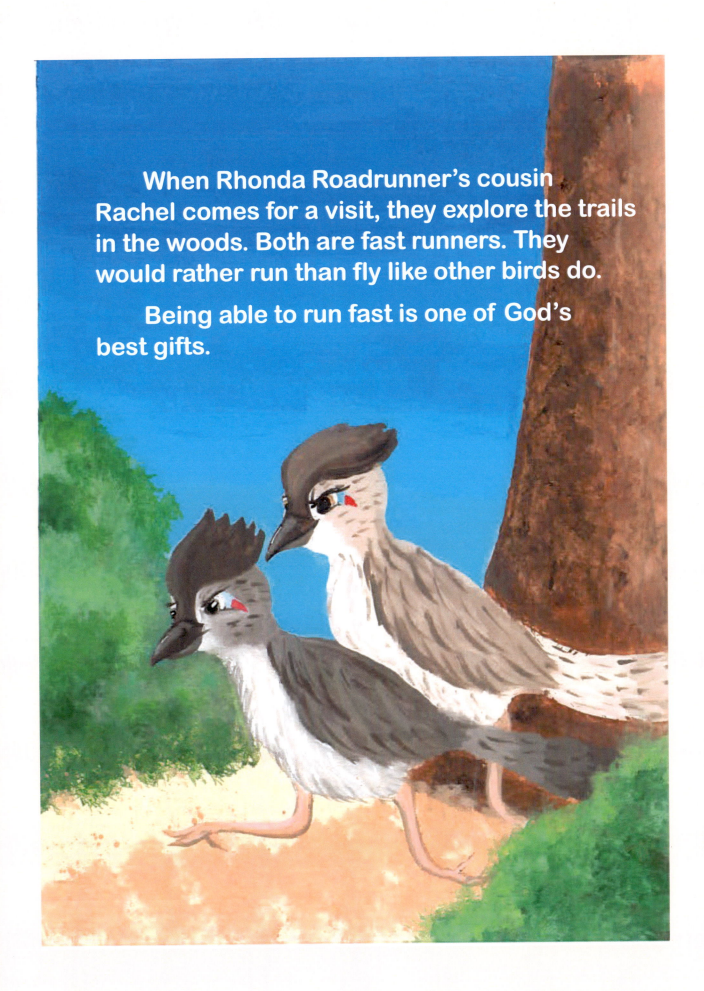

Randy Raccoon wears a black mask and has stripes on his long tail. He looks like he is dressed for Halloween. When Randy finds his food, he washes it with water from the stream that flows down the hillside.

Do you wash your hands before you eat breakfast?

Randy likes for his grandmother to visit. She is smart. She teaches Randy to be curious about things they find in a trash barrel.

God's gift of curiosity allows us to learn about the wonderful world He has made.

Suzi Squirrel is as cute as a button. She has dark eyes, fat little cheeks, and a gray tail that curls up like the letter "S." Suzi hunts for nuts and seeds and hides them until she is ready to eat.

What is your favorite food?

Suzi Squirrel plays tree-tag with her brother Sammy. They climb to the top of a tree and jump from one branch to another.

God has made squirrels better tree climbers than most of the animals.

Tommy Turtle lives in a hill country pond. On sunny days he sits on the grass and enjoys the sunshine. If someone walks nearby, Tommy pulls his head under his hard shell.

Do you like to play when the sun shines?

Tommy is a good swimmer. His aunt taught him to swim when he was a little turtle. Tommy can also hold his breath and swim under water for a long time.

God made some animals to live on land and some to live in water.

Benny Bat is a funny animal. He lives in a cave on the side of a hill. He sleeps hanging upside-down from the top of the cave. With his big ears, Benny can hear the softest sounds.

Can you hear your mother whispering?

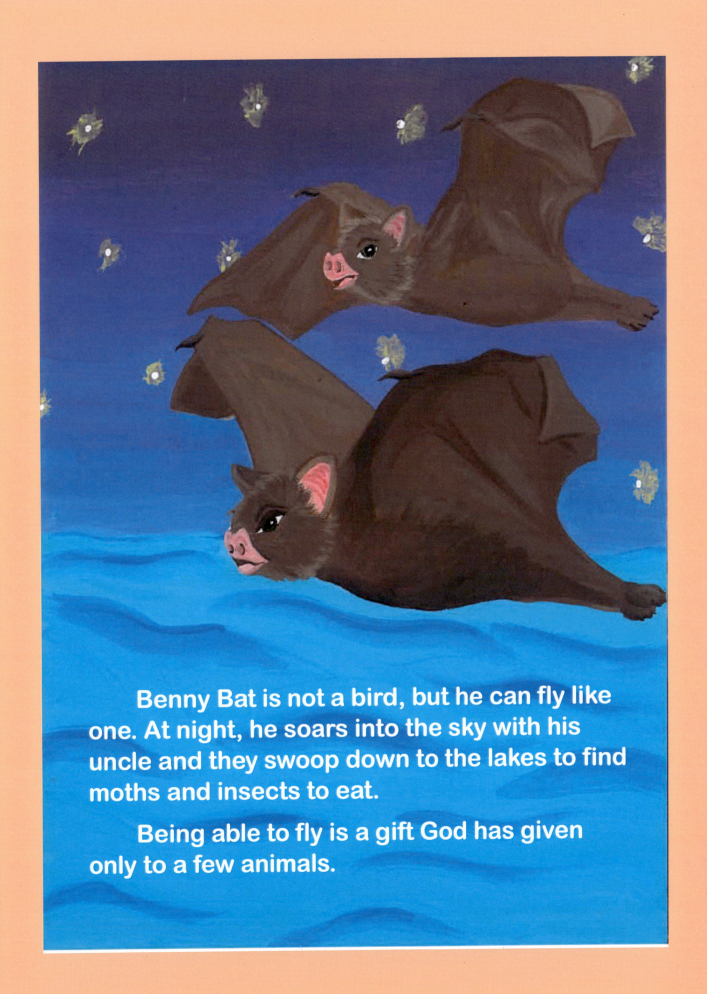

Benny Bat is not a bird, but he can fly like one. At night, he soars into the sky with his uncle and they swoop down to the lakes to find moths and insects to eat.

Being able to fly is a gift God has given only to a few animals.

Holly Javelina may look like a pig, but she is not one. Some people think Holly is not pretty because she has sharp teeth that stick out from her jaw, but do not tell that to her mother.

Does your mother think you are pretty?

Holly likes to eat cactus plants. Her mother has taught Holly how to tear a prickly-pear cactus apart and eat it like you would eat a peanut butter and jelly sandwich.

God has given all the animals good food to eat.

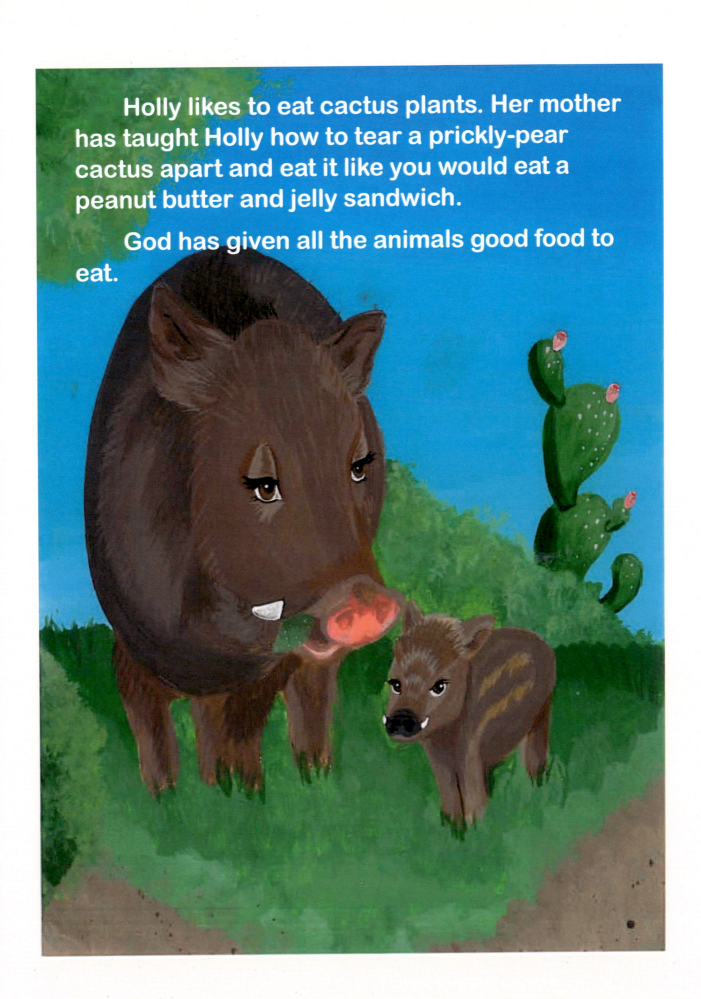

- How many animals can you find?
- Do you remember their names?
- What gift did God give each animal?

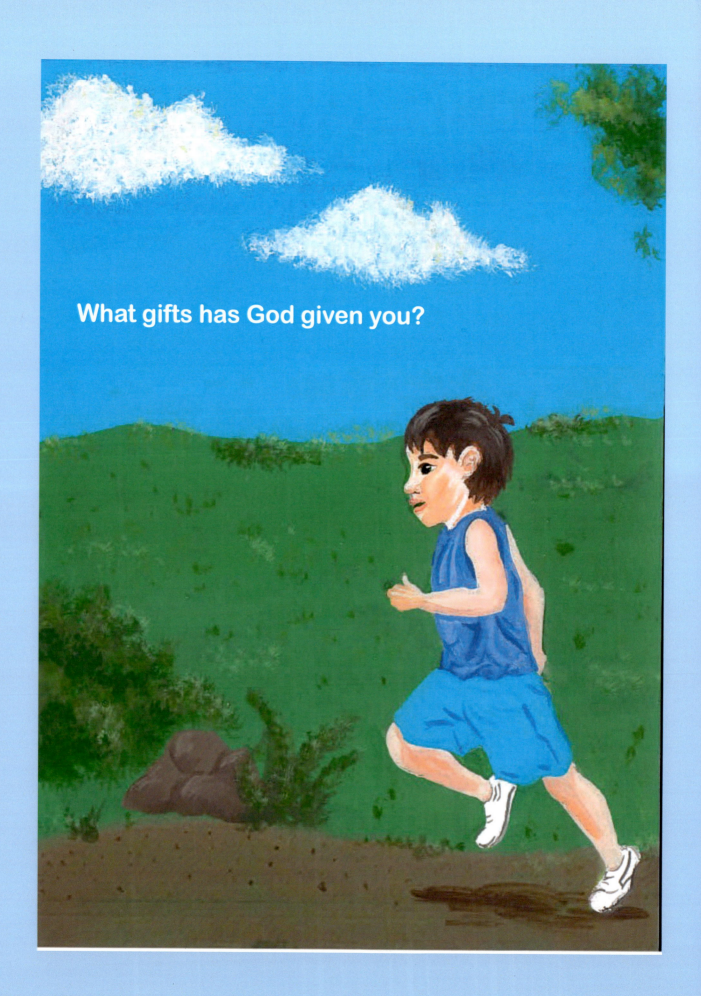

- Can you run?

- Can you jump?

- Does your family love you?